SAVANNAH RYAN

Abortion Facts: The American Experience With Truth

In the United States Roe vs Wade was enacted
in 1973, since that time more than 62 Million
abortions have happened in America.

In the year 2023 the Abortion count continues...

–ARCoA

Contents

1

Research And Statistics Sources

All information found in the book has been compiled from statistics by:

The Pew Research Center at https://www.pewresearch.org/

The Cable News Network (CNN) at https://www.cnn.com

Abort73 at https://abort73.com/abortion_facts/us_abortion_statistics/

Kff/org at https://www.kff.org/womens-health-policy

Ethics and Religious Liberty Commission at https://erlc.com/resource-library

USA Facts at https://usafacts.org/data/topics/people-society/health/maternal

The Guttmacher Institute at
https://www.guttmacher.org/united-states/abortion

Amnesty International at
https://www.amnesty.org/en/what-we-do/sexual

The Center For Disease Control (CDC) at
https://www.cdc.gov/reproductivehealth/data

Planned Parenthood at
https://www.plannedparenthood.org/learn/abortion/considering

2

What Is An Abortion

An abortion is the termination of a pregnancy before the fetus is able to survive outside the womb.

3

What The Types Of Abortions

The types of abortions are Medical and Surgical.

4

Worldwide Abortion Numbers

The number of abortions that occur worldwide each year is around 56 million.

5

What Countries Outlaw Abortions

These include El Salvador, Malta, Dominican Republic, Honduras, Nicaragua and the Vatican City

6

Where Is Abortion On Demand Legal

In Canada, Netherlands, Belgium, France, Germany, Spain, Sweden, United Kingdom, United States and China

7

When Did Abortions Begin In America

The history of abortion is complex and dates back to the colonial era.

8

Is Abortion Legal In The U.S.

Yes abortion is legal in all 50 states in the United States. However, the availability and accessibility of abortion services can vary greatly depending on the state.

In January 22, 1973 , Roe v. Wade affirmed the legality of a woman's right to have an abortion. On June 24, 2022 - The Supreme Court overturns Roe v. Wade holding that there is no longer a federal constitutional right to an abortion.

9

Where Are U.S. Abortions Performed

They perform abortions in clinics, hospitals, or private practices by licensed physicians, physician assistants and mid-wives.

Number Of Abortions In America Each Year

The estimated number of abortions in the United States is 862,320 each year

11

Are Abortions Safe

Abortion is considered to be safe when performed by a trained healthcare providers.

12

Are Abortions Dangerous

Risk of complications are generally low but can have lasting emotional and psychological effects.

13

Married vs Non-Married Abortion Rates

Nearly 85% of all abortions in America are performed on unmarried women, roughly 20% are performed on married women.

14

What Is Planned Parenthood

Planned Parenthood is one of the largest providers of reproductive health care services in the United States and performs roughly 300,000 to 350,000 abortions annually.

15

The Foundation Of Abortion In America

Margaret Sanger's views and methods were controversial in her time, and still are. Some criticized her for her views on eugenics and racist views. Sanger's activism and the birth control movement she started had a significant impact in the United States that continues until today.

16

How Many Facilities Provide Abortions Services In The U.S.

As of 2020 records, there were 1,603 facilities in the U.S. that provided abortions.

How Much Do Abortions Cost

U.S. abortions in the first trimester averaged $568 for a medication abortion and $625 for a procedural abortion. However in the second trimester the average cost rose to $775.

18

How Many Babies Survive The Abortion Process

The Centers for Disease Control and Prevention (CDC), reported only 7 babies survived the procedure in 2019.

Highest And Lowest Abortion Rates In America

The District of Columbia (Washington D.C.) has the highest abortion rate in America, while Missouri has the lowest abortion rate of all States within the U.S.

20

Whats The Earliest An Abortion Can Be Performed

Some states have laws that ban abortions as early as 6 weeks.

21

Whats The Latest An Abortion Can Be Peformed

Roughly 20 states ban abortions after a certain point in pregnancy, such as 20 weeks.

22

What Age Range Has The Highest Abortion Rates

Women in there 20's accounted for (57%) of all abortions in America.

What Education Level Has The Most Abortions

Women with some college or associate degrees account for nearly 41% of all abortions in the U.S.

24

Abortion Complication Statistics

Only 2% of all abortions in the U.S. involve some type of complication for the woman.

Death Of Women During Abortions

From 1973 to 2019 the (CDC) reported 525 women died due to complications from legal abortion.

26

White Women And Abortion

White women comprised 39% of abortion recipients in the U.S.

27

Black Women And Abortion

Black women comprised 28% of abortion recipients in the U.S.

28

Hispanic Women Abortions

Hispanic women comprised 25% of abortion recipients in the U.S.

29

Asian Women Abortions

Asian women comprised 6% of abortion recipients in the U.S.

30

Minor vs Parents And Abortions

40% of minors reported having an abortion without parental consent.

31

Repeat Abortion Statistics

Nearly 42% of women who had an abortion in 2019 had previously had at least one abortion.

32

Abortion And Religion

Nearly 54% of women who had an abortion identify with a Christian faith.

33

Abortion And Wealth

49% of all abortions in the U.S. are performed on women who live below the Federal poverty level.

The Abortion Debate And Choice

Abortion should remain a personal choice because it is a deeply personal and complex issue that can be influenced by a wide range of factors, including a person's physical, emotional, and financial well-being.

A woman's right to make decisions about her own body and reproductive health is a fundamental aspect of her autonomy and privacy.

Additionally, criminalizing or restricting access to abortion can have negative consequences for women's health and well-being, and can disproportionately affect marginalized and low-income communities.

www.ingramcontent.com/pod-product-compliance
Lightning Source LLC
Chambersburg PA
CBHW051716250726
48653CB00007B/3059